A CONNECTICUT YANKEE IN KING ARTHUR'S COURT

the notebook edition

Colour the Classics xoxo

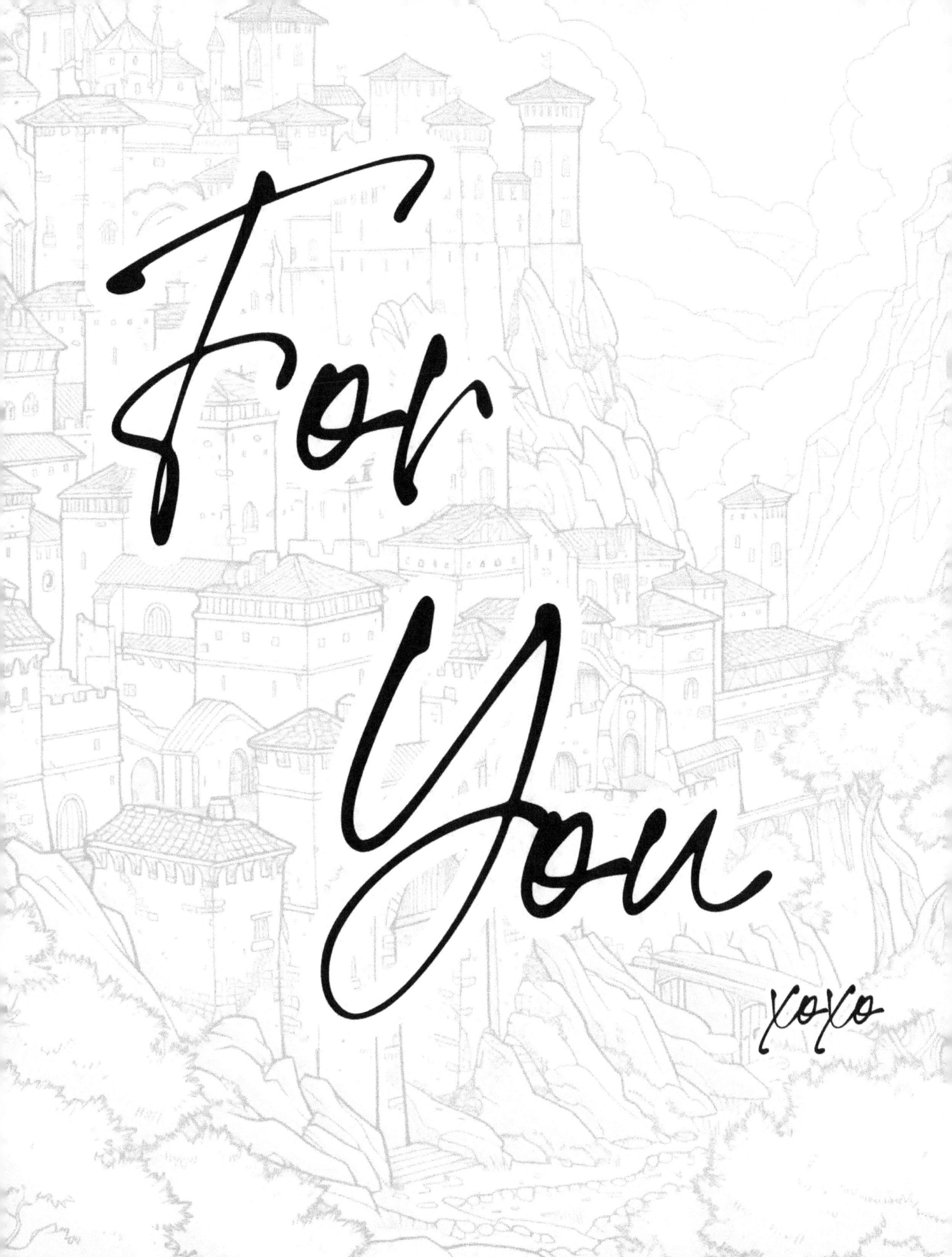
For You
xoxo

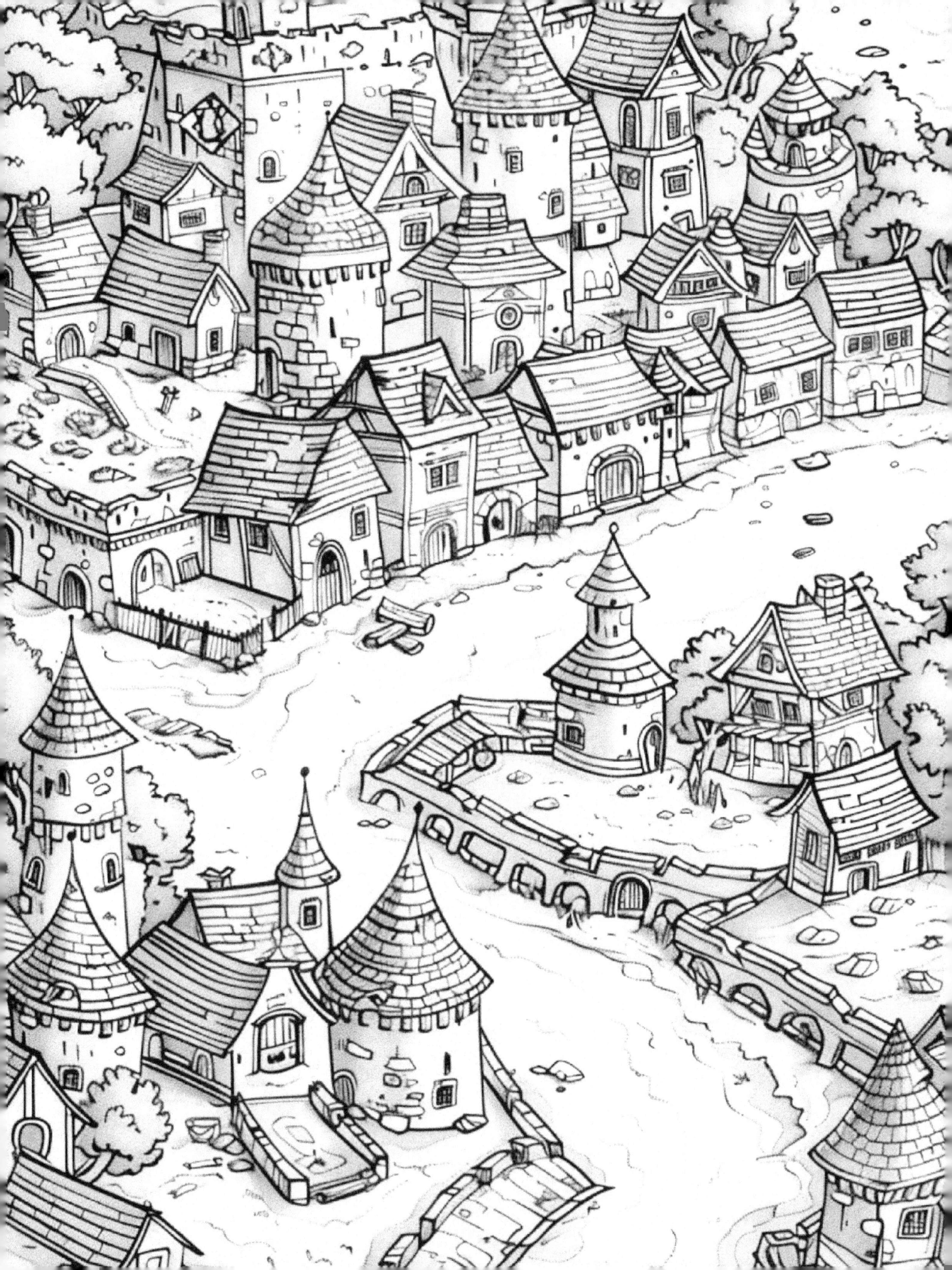

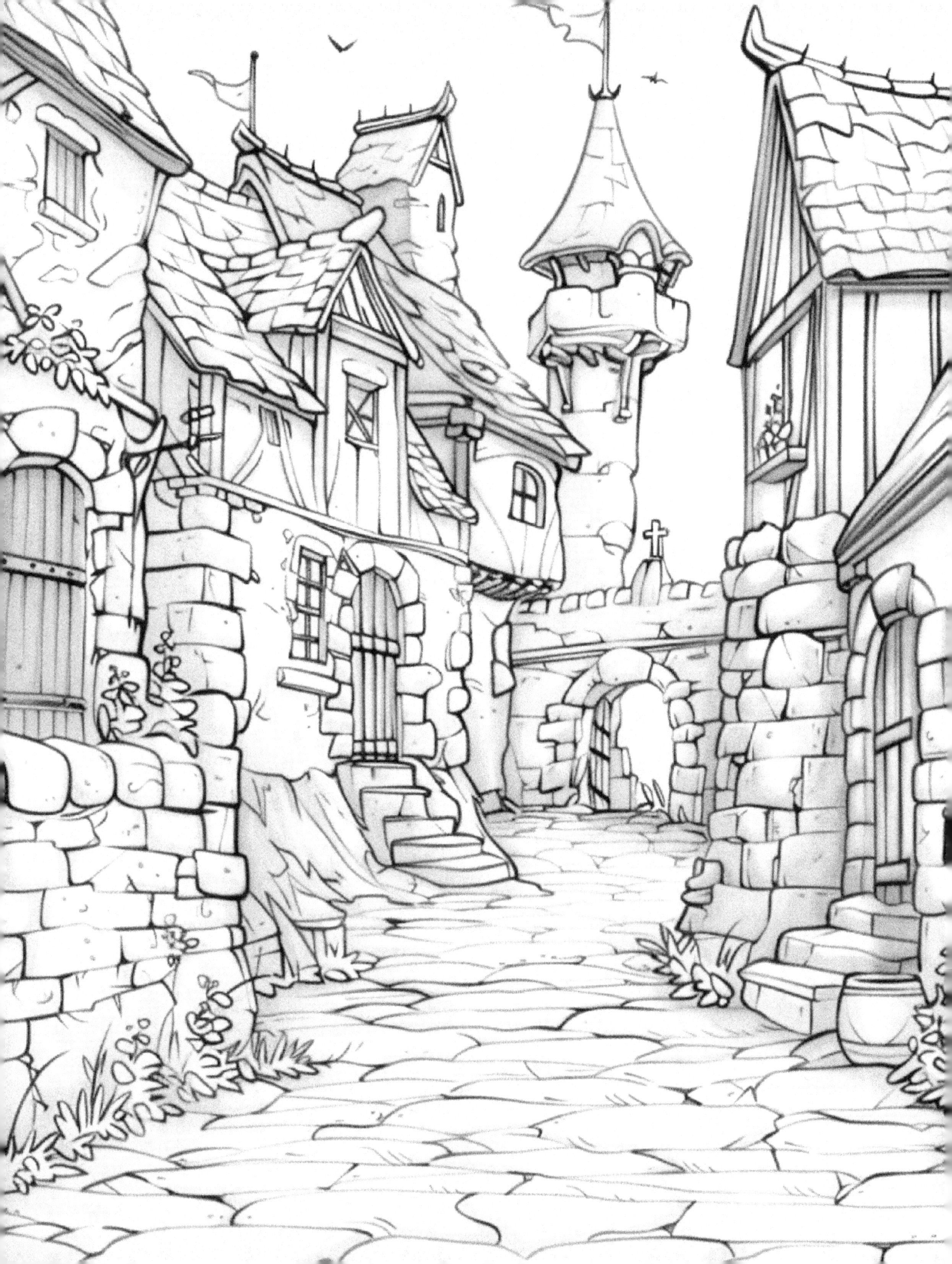

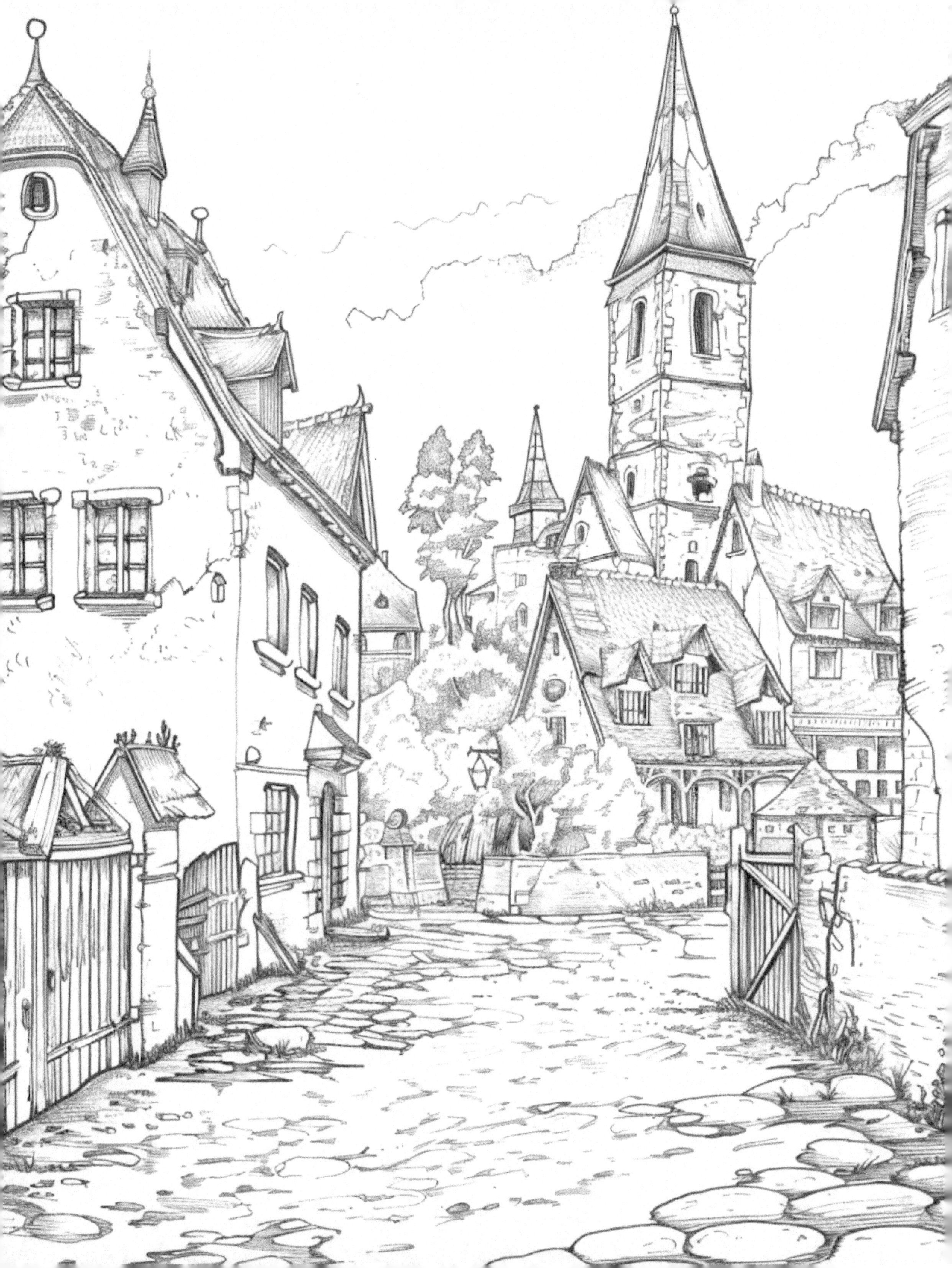

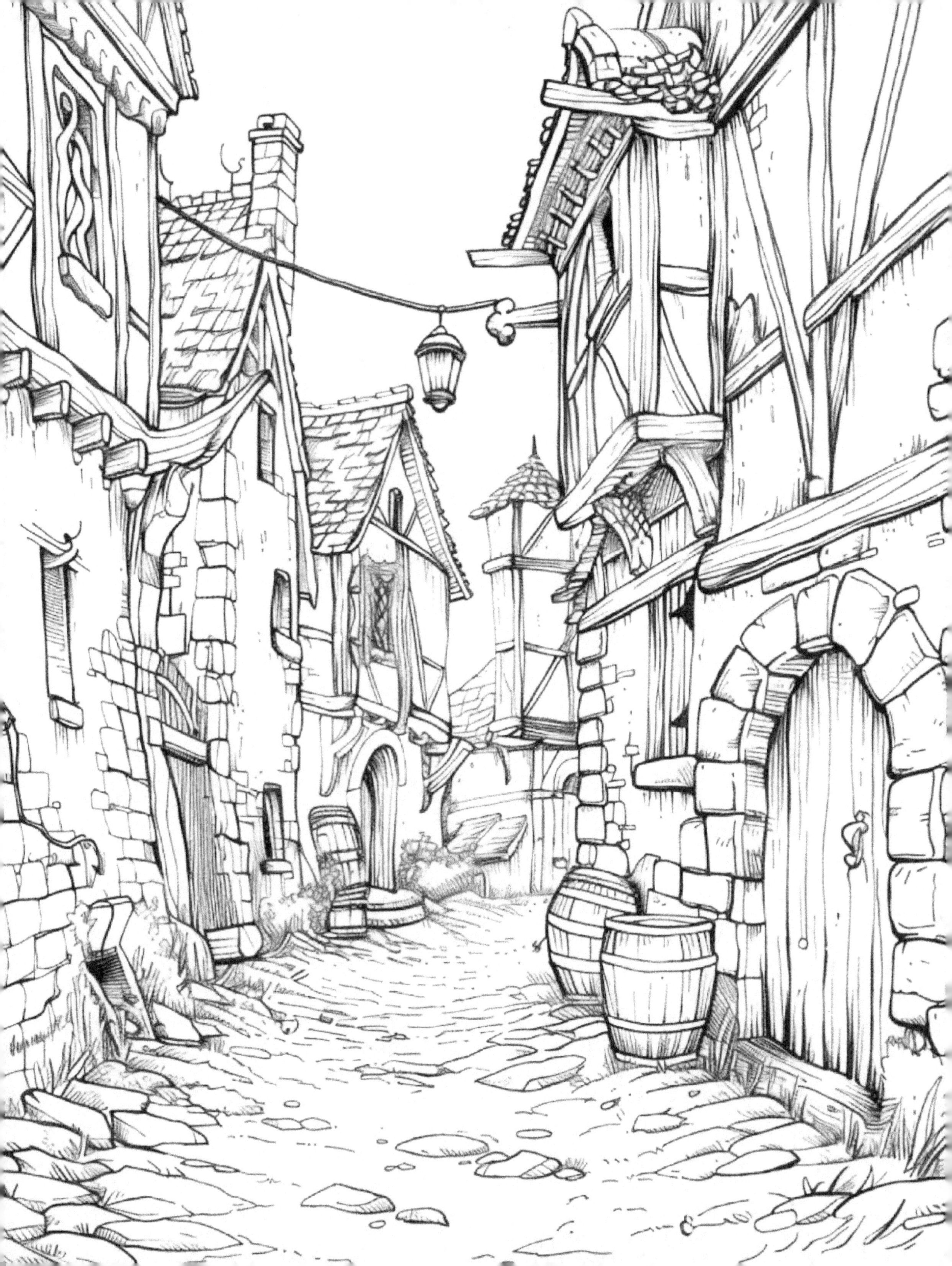

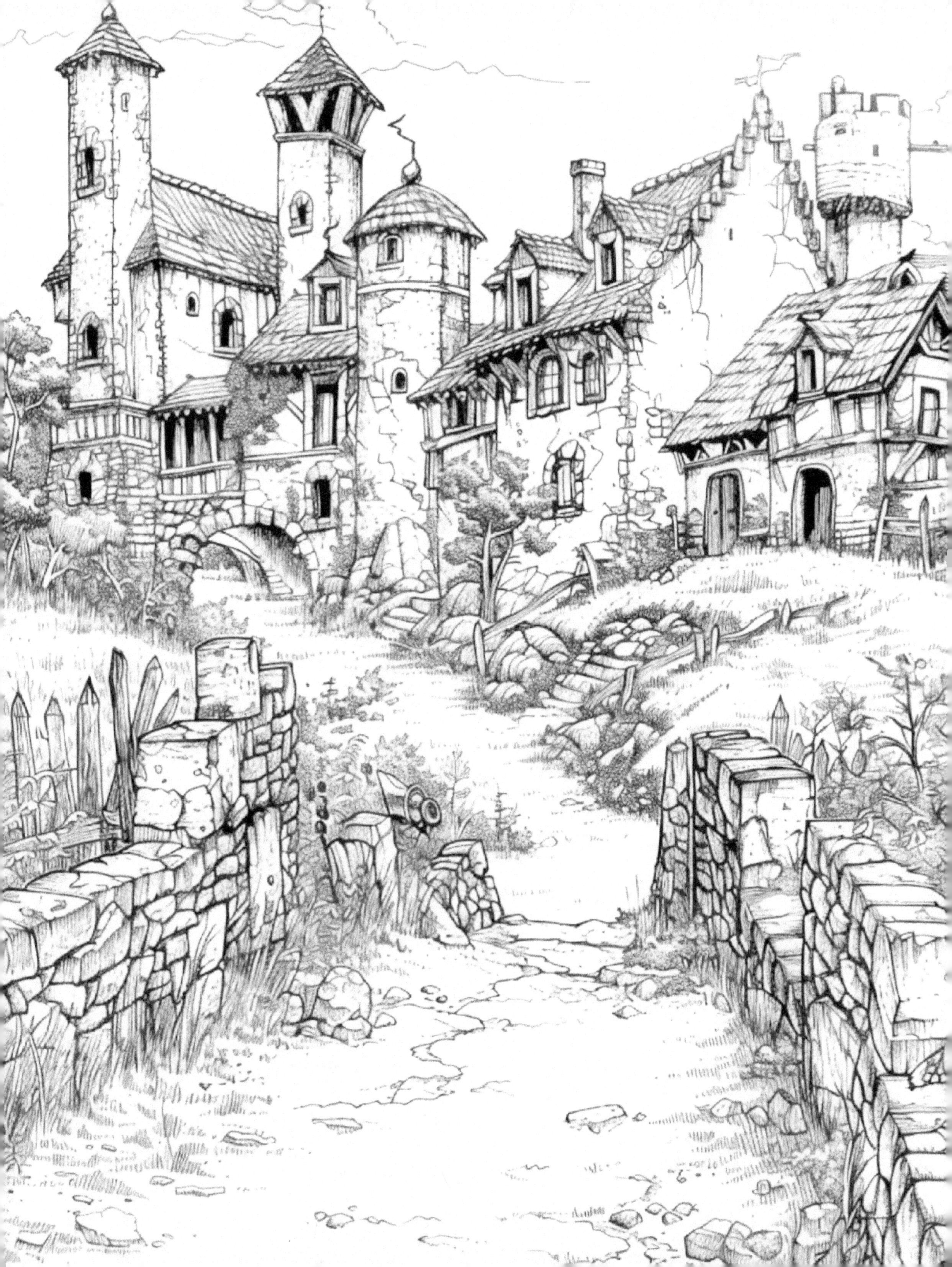

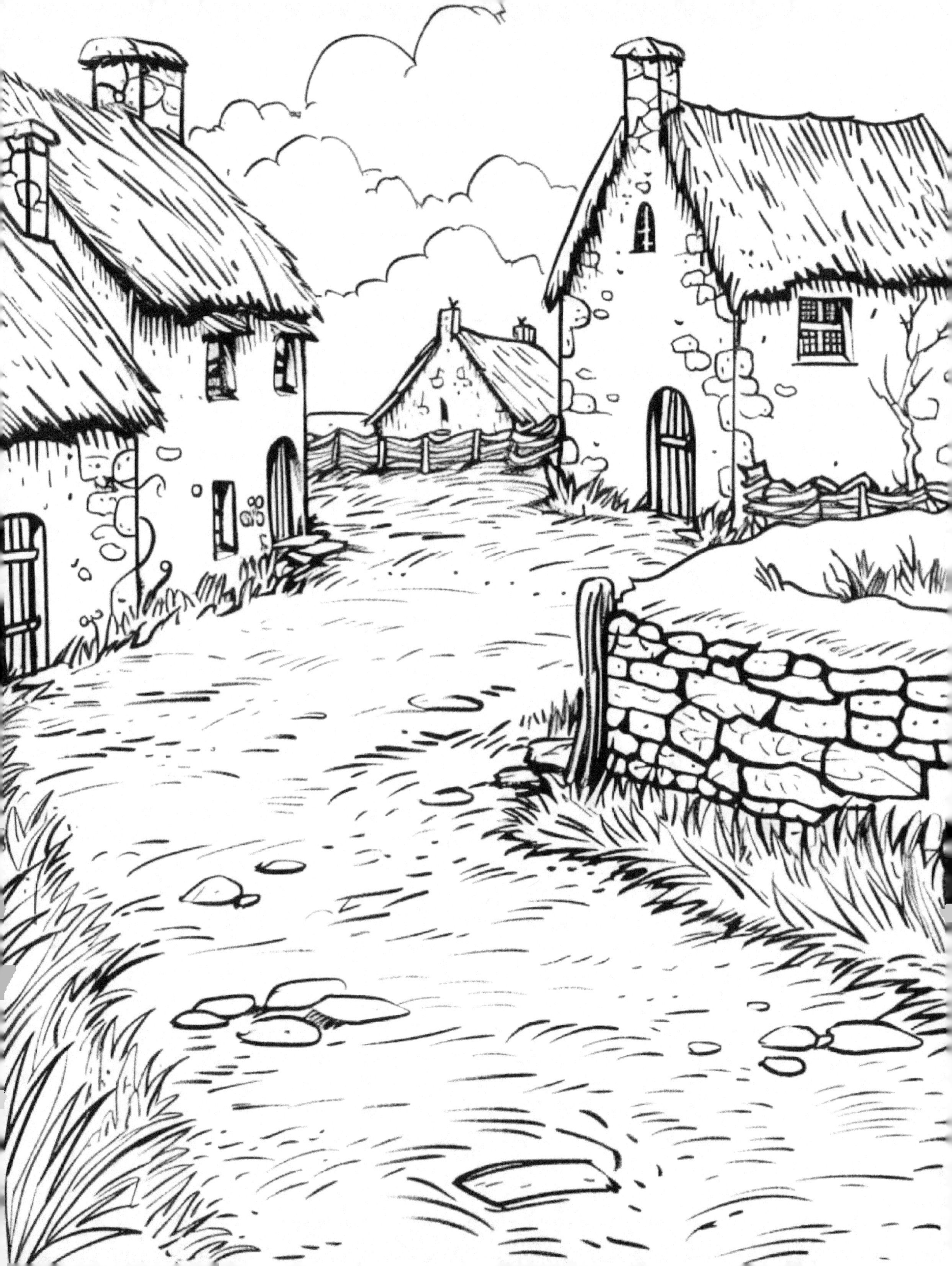

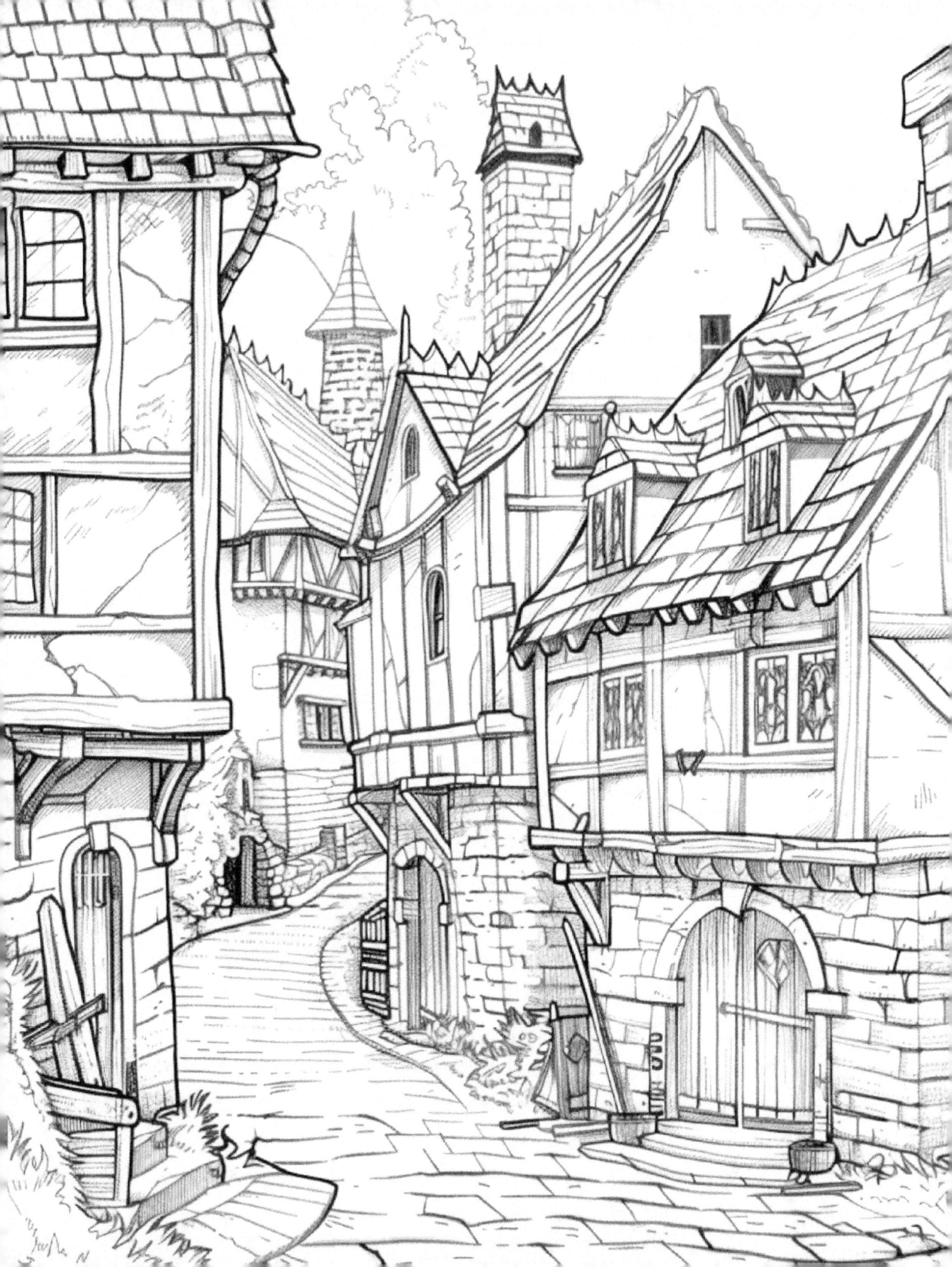

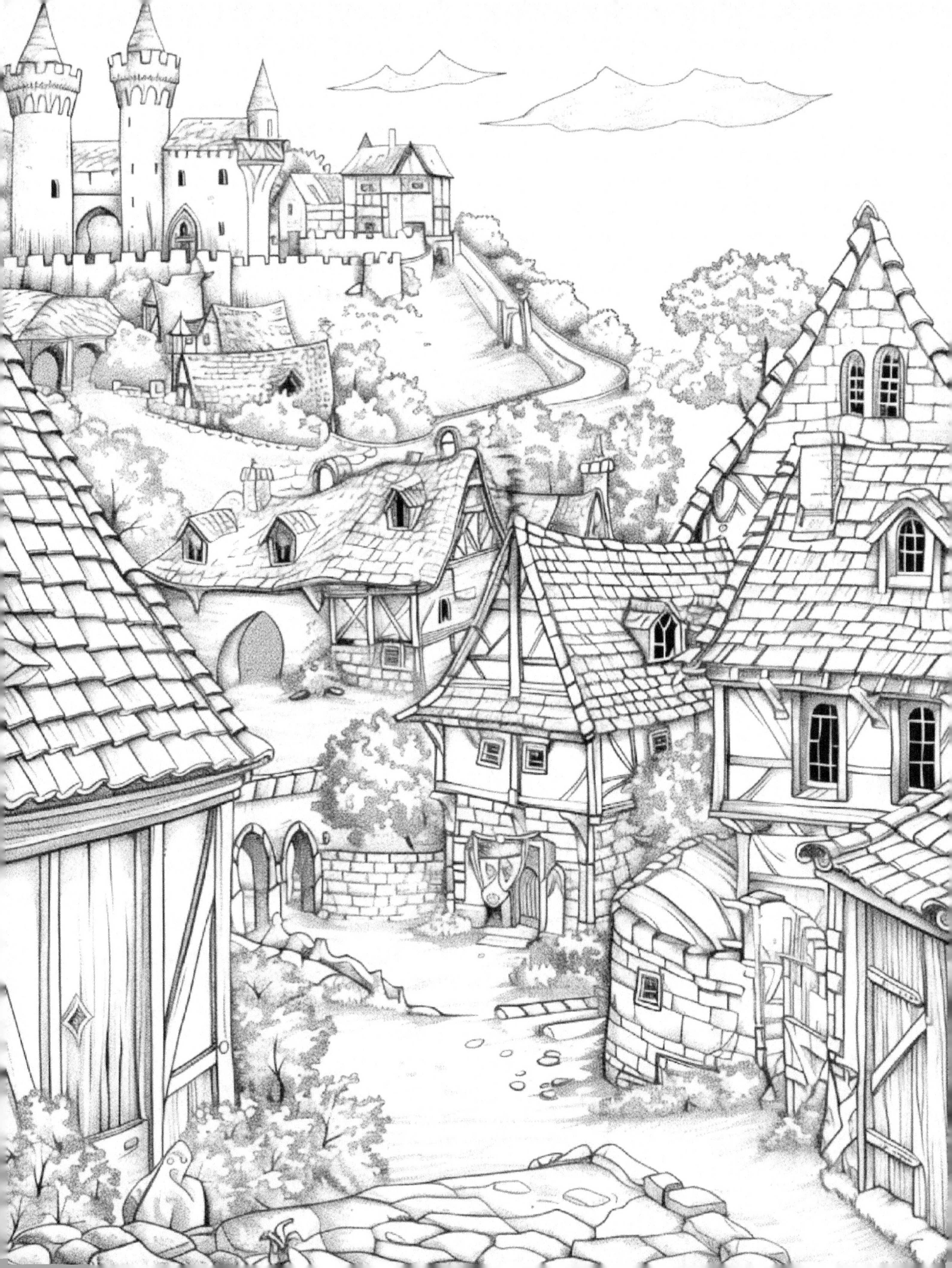

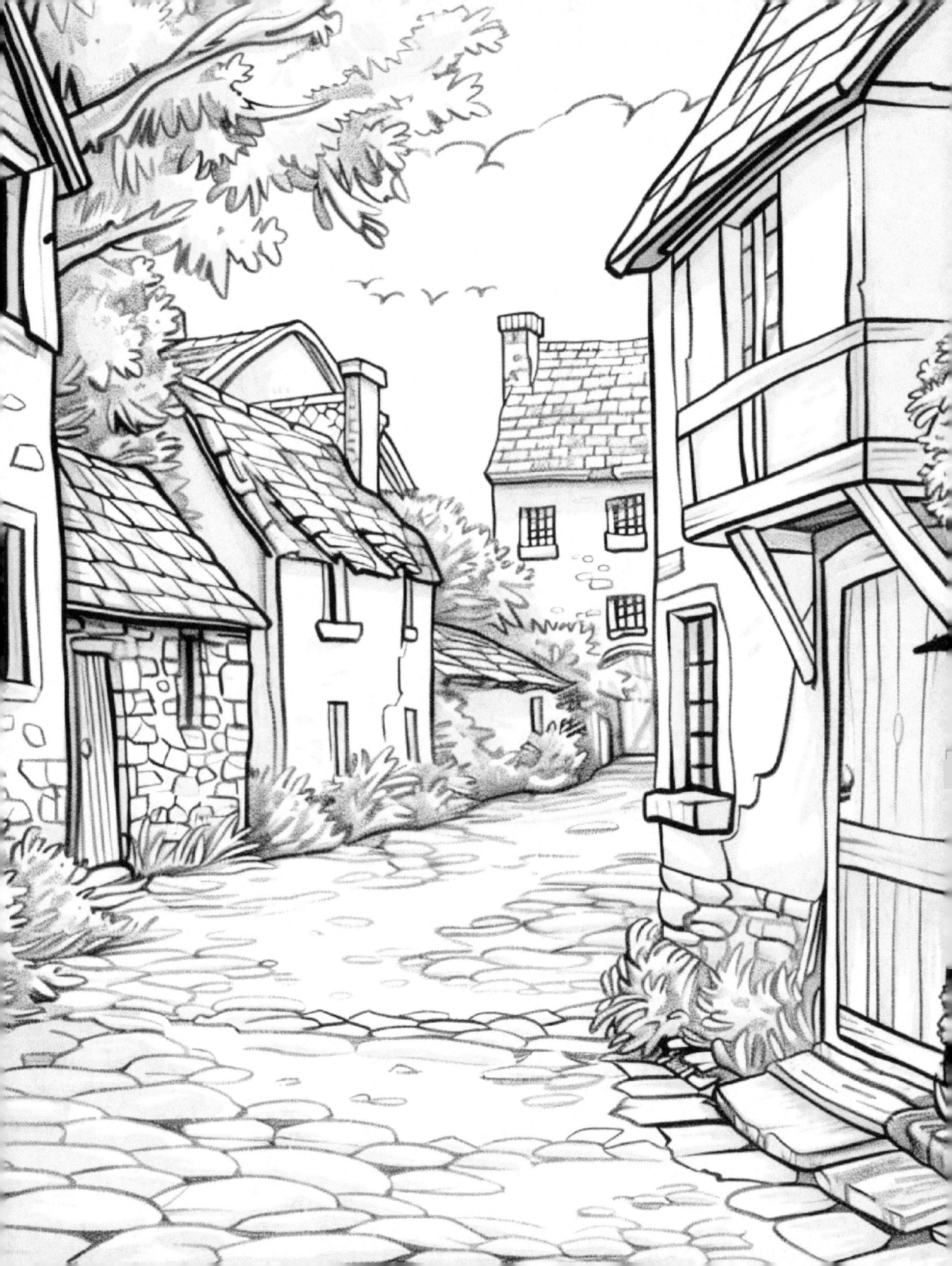

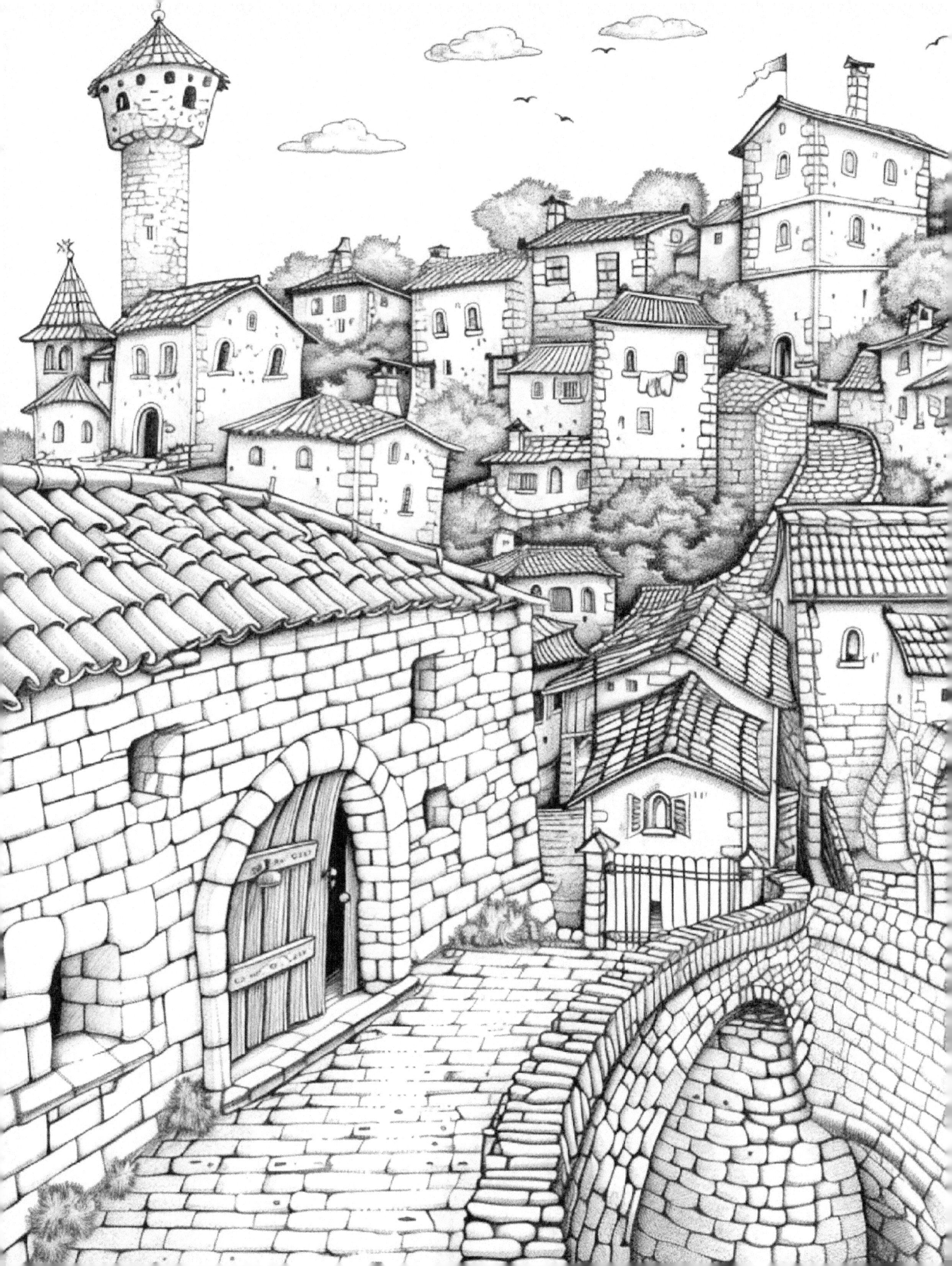

The End

Follow us:

@colourtheclassics